NIGHT IN A WOOD CABIN

Wálé Akíngbadé

Illustrated by
Olivia Brook-Alfa

Copyrighted Material

Night In A Wood Cabin
Copyright © 2024 by Wálé Akíngbadé / Think GTI Ltd.
All Rights Reserved

The moral right of the author has been asserted

No part of this publication may be reproduced, stored in a retrieval system or transmitted, in any form or by any means— electronic, mechanical, photocopying, recording or otherwise— without prior written permission from the publisher, except for the inclusion of brief quotations in a review.

For information about this title or to order other books and/or electronic media, contact the publisher:

Think GTI Ltd
distribution@thinkgti.com
www.thinkgti.com

ISBN-13: 978-1-0686543-2-9 (Paperback Edition)
ISBN-13: 978-1-0686543-3-6 (Hardcover edition)

A story about embracing uncertainty

Scan the QR code to listen to accompanying soundtrack.

In 'Night in a Wood Cabin', a second story in the 'Golden Threads of Inspiration' series, readers are drawn into a captivating exploration of courage and self-discovery. Set against the backdrop of an enchanting forest, the story follows Nia, a young adventurer on a quest for meaning and purpose. As she navigates the unknown, Nia learns to embrace uncertainty as a catalyst for growth, confronting her fears and uncovering hidden strengths along the way.

Through the challenges of the forest, Nia discovers the transformative power of self-belief and resilience through introspection. 'Night in a Wood Cabin' is a timeless tale that reminds readers of the importance of embracing uncertainty, trusting in ourselves, and embracing the unknown terrains of life and the circumstances it presents with self-assurance, courage and determination.

Night In A Wood Cabin

For my dear mother, sisters, my niece and friends who through their strength of character, adventurous spirit and curiousity inspired the key attributes of the main character of this story.

"Ile ti ko ti oju eni su, okunkun re soro irin."
- Yorubá Proverb

Translation:
It is difficult to navigate at night (or in the dark) a new terrain that one had not yet explored in the light of day

CONTENTS

9.

RESTLESS ROOTS

19

INTO THE UNKNOWN

29

WHISPERS AND SONGS

37

THE CABIN

45

SHADOWS AND SILENCE

57
MIND'S LABYRINTH

71
LIGHT IN THE CLEARING

83
THE MERCHANT'S LESSON

101
RETURN TO THE VILLAGE

chapter one

I

restless roots

Night In A Wood Cabin

Nia stood at the edge of the woods, heart heavy with longing for something beyond the narrow paths and familiar voices of her village. The winding roads of Ilé-Ifẹ̀ once full of wonder, now felt too small for the questions brewing within her. The bustling marketplace, where traders shouted over ripe plantains and spiced groundnuts, no longer stirred excitement. Instead, it echoed the sameness of days she'd begun to outgrow.

Since childhood, she'd been drawn to the rarely trodden paths in the forest surrounding her village. Where others saw danger, she saw mystery. Where the elders told cautionary tales, Nia heard an invitation to explore. The stories passed from mouth to mouth were of shape-shifters, monstrous beasts, enchanted trees, but these only fed her curiosity. Under the glow of the moonlight, children would gather by the fireside, joining in the choruses of old songs that echoed ancestral lore. Nia had always lingered on the parts others found frightening. She listened intently not to the warnings, but to the unspoken possibilities that lay ahead.

As a girl, Nia would wander to the outskirts of the village, often escaping her chores to peer beyond the known regions. The tall trees there seemed to wave to her, whispering riddles on the

wind. It was during one of these ventures that she first saw the towering Uloko Tree, majestic and unlike any other. She'd lost her way that day but found something greater: a sense of herself she had never known.

That moment stayed with her, etched deep in her memory. As the years passed, so did the rhythm of life in the village, predictable and well-worn. Yet Nia's spirit remained restless, pulled by dreams of distant trails, unseen lands, and stories yet untold.

She wasn't afraid of the monsters others feared. If anything, she believed she could outwit, could outclimb, outrun, outthink any creature the forest launched at

Night In A Wood Cabin

her. She imagined herself not as the frightened victim in tales, but the daring protagonist who confronted threats with courage and wit. The night held no terror for her, only potential.

And now, standing once again where the forest met the village, she gazed beyond the line of trees. The breeze stirred her dress, and the tall grass shifted in a soft rhythm. Something in the air felt different, like an unseen invitation calling her forward.

The stories of her village had shaped her curiosity, but her path would soon shape her story.

One day as a young girl, Nia got lost whilst on an errand from her garndmother to pluck wild herbs from the edge of the forest. She got carried away wandering, before realising she had been walking in circles.

She looked up, trying to determine the sun's position. 'The sun helps lost travellers find their bearings,' she had learnt from folklore. Still, the trees around her had blocked the sky, so she sought one suitable for climbing to glance above the towering forest canopy.

It was then that she found an unusually tall tree. "If I climb this tree, I'll get a glance above all the other, then I will be able to see the sun to get my bearings to find a route home."

She did so and found the route back to her home. When she arrived, she told everyone about the tall tree that helped her find her way!

The word spread quickly accross the small town and everyone soon knew of the tall tree that the local people would eventually refer to as the Uloko tree.

chapter two
II

into the unknown

Night In A Wood Cabin

The forest had always called to Nia. Its mysteries were a quiet hum beneath the daily rhythms of village life. As a young girl, Nia had first wandered into the woods during an afternoon on an errand from her grandmother to fetch some ewé egbessin, special leaves she used for preparing batches of akara and moi-moi she would sell at the market.

Young Nia got lost and then stumbled upon the Uloko Tree, a towering presence in the woods. Climbing it not only helped find her way home but also gave her a view of the vast lands beyond the confines of her village. That moment stayed with her, shaping the way she saw the world.

Now older, her curiosity had deepened into something restless. With every passing season, the confines of Ilé-Ifè grew tighter, like a garment she had outgrown. She yearned for discovery, not just of places, but of parts of herself she could not yet name. The villagers clung to tradition and repetition, but Nia was made of questions and wonder.

One market day, amid the commotion of bartering voices and wafting aromas of pepper stew and moi-moi, she made her quiet escape. With her backpack slung firmly over her shoulder, she followed the dirt path towards the tree line. It was the perfect moment—no one would notice her absence until the sun was well on its descent.

As she passed the familiar edge of the village, the air seemed to shift. The forest greeted her like an old friend, the kind whose silence said more than words. The trees whispered in a tongue only her spirit could understand. The wind moved gently through the leaves, but now the shadows felt deeper, the sunlight more fractured.

She stepped carefully, her feet tracing paths she'd only imagined. Her eyes scanned the forest floor, mapping subtle signs: the direction of moss on bark, the angle of branches leaning toward the sun. Every bird's call and every rustle held meaning. She moved with a confidence born not of experience, but of intuition.

Still, the forest was unfamiliar in its vastness. The deeper she ventured, the more it seemed to change around her. Trees stood taller, their roots like fingers curled around secrets buried deep beneath the soil. The canopy thickened, filtering sunlight into gold-dappled patches. Strange clusters of mushrooms glowed faintly in the shade, and vines coiled like silent sentinels along the bark.

Though she was not afraid, she could feel the stories of her childhood rising from her memory; whispered warnings of creatures that hunted under moonlight, of shadows that moved with minds of their own. But she shook them off. She was here now, forging her own tale.

She marked trees with etched symbols as she moved, a breadcrumb trail of her presence. The forest responded in kind—birds sang in sharper tones, insects fluttered with a peculiar rhythm, and even the light seemed to shift in tandem with her breath.

At one point, a branch snapped sharply behind her. Nia froze. She turned, heart thudding. Nothing. Just a squirrel dashing across the underbrush. Yet the

Night In A Wood Cabin

moment lingered longer than it should have.

She whispered aloud, almost playfully, "I see you, forest. I feel your eyes."

The wind picked up slightly, brushing her cheeks with a cool touch, as if answering her challenge. It was the first sign that the forest would not just be a backdrop to her adventure, but an active participant.

And so she walked on, deeper into the unknown, where every path ahead promised discovery and every sound behind held mystery.

chapter three

III

whispers and songs

Night In A Wood Cabin

It was a sound both strange and familiar, a whistle drifting faintly through the forest canopy. Nia paused mid-step, her ears straining to catch its rhythm. The melody stirred memories from her village, from one of the old tales her grandmother used to tell. It was a song from the legend of Oluronbi, the tale of a shamed barren woman, who in her desperation for a child, vowed to give up the child to the Uloko, only if she would be granted one.

Guided by the melody, she followed its echo until she emerged into a clearing. There, standing with his back to her, was another traveller. He wore a patterned tunic of unfamiliar weave. His presence felt out of place.

Nia paused before greeting him, unsure whether to step forward or retreat. The stranger turned slowly, his eyes kind, his smile unhurried. There was a calmness about him, like a man who'd walked many roads and had little left to prove.

She hesitated, then asked the question that had been circling her mind. "How do you know that song? It's from my village. Are you… a merchant?" she asked, her voice barely above a whisper.

He nodded gently. "From the Southlands," he said, brushing a speck of dust from his sleeve. "But I trade in more than just goods."

Nia tilted her head. "Then what else do you trade?"

"Stories," he replied with a glint in his eye. "They travel faster than anything I carry."

He chuckled softly. "Stories are like wind. They weave through lands, carried by tongues and memory." The merchant spoke of places beyond Ilé-Ifè, of market squares where the scent of spices filled the air, of trees that bore fruit even when no one watched. When he spoke of the Uloko Tree, he called it something else — Iroko — a name from his homeland, spoken with reverence. Nia listened, entranced.

He told her of his younger self, a boy with restless feet and a head full of borrowed stories.

"The forest tests everyone," he said, reflecting on his own story as he gazed into the distance. "But it rewards those who listen more than they speak."

He offered her a carved tablet, a map, etched with trails and symbols. "There's a cabin," he said, tapping a spot marked with an 'x'. "It's safe, and near. You'll need shelter tonight. The forest changes with the dark."

She hesitated. "Why help me?"
"Because someone once helped me, too." he replied simply.

Before parting ways, he gave her a final piece of advice: "The journey teaches more than the destination. Rest when you must, but never stop listening."

chapter four

IV

Night In A Wood Cabin

Night In A Wood Cabin

Nia stepped towards the cabin as marked on the map, her thoughts turning over the merchant's words. Who was he really? A traveller? A guide? Or something more mysterious?

Only the forest knew.

The cabin appeared slowly, almost shyly, between the trees. Its edges blended into the forest until the final turn revealed it fully. A humble structure of dark wood and sloping roof, with smoke curling gently from a clay chimney.

Nia's heart lifted slightly. For all its mystery, it looked welcoming. She stepped closer, noting the careful details:

the hand-carved lintel, the curtain of vines draping the entrance, the gentle creak of the swinging door. It seemed to breathe with the forest.

Inside, warmth greeted her. A low fire crackled in the hearth. Shelves lined the walls, filled with unfamiliar tools, gourds, and wooden trinkets. A cot sat against one side, covered in woven blankets dyed in hues of indigo and ochre. The aroma of dried herbs hung in the air.

On the table lay a wooden bowl filled with ripe forest fruits. A note etched into a carved tablet simply read: "Rest. Eat. Reflect. Depart only when ready."

She sat slowly, drinking in the silence. Her hands trembled slightly, not from fear, but the aftershock of transition. She had crossed a threshold, and this place was neither village nor wilderness. It was something else, suspended between who she was and who she would become.

Outside, dusk deepened. Shadows lengthened into unfamiliar shapes. The comforting noises of the forest were replaced by creaks and groans, whispering through branches and leaves.

Nia began to feel the weight of uncertainty press in. Every sound was

amplified. Every flicker of light cast ominous silhouettes. Her heartbeat kept rhythm with the ticking of unseen branches tapping the roof.

She lay on the cot, eyes wide open, listening. The wind changed direction. A branch scraped the window. Then silence. Then a thump. Her body tensed.

In the hush that followed, she heard a quiet whisper not from outside, but from within herself. A question echoing softly: "What have you come here to find?" She didn't yet have an answer. But she knew the forest would help her uncover it.

Darkness settled thickly around the cabin, a weight more felt than seen. Nia sat upright on the cot, her senses heightened by the silence that blanketed everything. The soft crackling of the hearth-fire was no longer comforting. Instead, it flickered ominously, casting long, jagged shadows across the walls.

Every creak in the timber, every groan of the wind outside became a whisper of uncertainty. She had grown up hearing tales of monsters that emerged when the moon rose, beasts that prowled the edges of sanity and turned shadows into weapons. Now those stories seemed less like folklore and more like prophecy.

chapter five

V

shadows and
silence

Night In A Wood Cabin

A sudden gust of wind slammed the wooden shutter against the cabin wall. Nia jumped. Her breath caught in her throat, and her pulse quickened.

The wind howled like a mourning spirit, dragging its fingers along the eaves, rattling the door latch as if trying to enter.

She pulled the blanket tighter around her shoulders, but it could not ward off the creeping sense of dread. Her thoughts began to spiral, replaying the stranger's words. "The forest changes with the dark." What did he mean? Was he warning her of something more than rustling leaves and howling wind?

Outside, twigs snapped. Something or someone was moving.

Nia crept to the window, her breath fogging the glass. In the faint moonlight, a figure shifted between trees. Not quite visible, not quite hidden. She rubbed her eyes, certain she must be imagining it, but there it was again: a flicker of movement, like a shadow detaching itself from the dark.

Panic surged in her chest. Her mind reached for explanations. Could it be bandits, forest animals, or even spirits? Her rational mind wrestled with fear, but it was losing the battle.

Another thud. This time from the roof.

She stood frozen, her eyes darting to the corners of the room. The once-inviting cabin now felt like a trap, a wooden box surrounded by a forest alive with whispers and unseen intentions.

Then came what sounded like footsteps.

Slow. Deliberate. Just beyond the walls. A floorboard creaked inside the cabin. But she hadn't moved.

Nia spun around, heart pounding. Nothing there. Yet the air had become heavier now, thicker, as though the room itself was holding its breath.

She reached for the carved map the merchant had given her. Its edges felt smooth beneath her fingers, grounding her. "This place is a resting ground," she whispered to herself, trying to steady her thoughts. "It is safe. It is safe."

But the forest outside disagreed. Another gust of wind pushed open the door slightly, revealing only a sliver of the darkness beyond. And in that space, just for a second, she thought she saw eyes staring back.

Her instincts screamed for her to flee, but her legs refused to move. She closed the door quickly and bolted it, breathing hard. Every tale she'd heard

as a child returned in waves, of shape-shifters, cursed travellers, and ancient spirits that lingered in the woods.

What if the merchant had tricked her? What if this cabin wasn't a sanctuary, but a lure by a deceptive werewolf?

She crouched by the fire, wrapping herself in silence. The crackle of flames echoed loudly in her ears, as if mocking her fear. The shadows danced more wildly now, playing across the walls like spectres in a twisted play. Eventually, her fear exhausted itself. Her mind, though still restless, was calmer. The cabin door stayed shut, and no creature burst through the walls.

Still, even as her eyes grew heavy, sleep did not come easily. Somewhere, a branch cracked once more. Somewhere, footsteps faded into the distance. But whether they were real or imagined, Nia could not be certain.

Between bouts of drowsy drifts, she slipped into a dream where she saw herself confronting a dragon, armed with just a torch to defend her beloved fellow villagers.

In her dream, the brighter the light of her torch shone, the smaller the dragon got until it completely dwindled in size and fluttered away like a fly.

Night In A Wood Cabin

chapter six
VI

mind's labyrinth

Nia was suddenly awoken by a knock, and the startle reminded her that the forest had only just begun to test her.

The embers in the fireplace hearth had dimmed to a dull glow by the time Nia opened her eyes again. She didn't remember falling asleep, but her neck ached from where she had slumped, curled tightly on the cot. A vague unease still clung to her skin, like the remnants of the dream she couldn't shake. But it wasn't a dream—not entirely.

The wind had calmed, but the silence was now deafening, thick and weighty.

Something about it felt unnatural,

like the forest was holding its breath, watching.

Nia sat up, ears attuned to the smallest sounds. Every creak in the wooden frame seemed louder now. Her senses were sharp, her thoughts racing, yet something within her resisted clarity. Was it tiredness? Or was it the forest pressing deeper into her mind?

She stood slowly and approached the window again. Nothing. Just the trees standing still in the softest shimmer of moonlight. But something gnawed at her, unseen but undeniably present.

She looked around the room. Everything was in its place. And yet… everything also felt slightly off.

A sense of displacement began to take root. The fireplace, the wooden beams, the carved decorations, she wondered if they always looked like this? She couldn't tell anymore. Had the merchant mentioned anything about strange occurrences at night? Her memory betrayed her now, fragments of their conversation scattering like dry leaves in her mind.

The shadows in the corners had grown longer, darker and almost sentient. She could swear they twitched when she

wasn't looking directly at them. One moment, the chair stood empty. Next, she thought she saw a figure sitting in it, only for it to vanish when she turned her head.

Her mind was becoming a battlefield, and she was losing ground.

She pressed her fingers to her temples, trying to anchor herself. "This is just fear," she whispered. "Just a trick of the night." But the doubt inside her refused to settle.

There was another knock.

It was soft, so faint she almost convinced

herself it hadn't happened.

Then three knocks again, slow and deliberate, like someone toying with her fear.

Nia froze. The door was still bolted. She hadn't heard footsteps. There were no shadows approaching from outside—only the knocks, echoing now in her skull.

She didn't move. Couldn't.

Her breath grew shallow, her heartbeat deafening in her ears. She began to doubt her own senses. Had she imagined it all? Or was something standing there… waiting?

She stepped back, one foot at a time, as if any sudden movement would provoke something unseen. Her hand brushed against the carved map the merchant had given her—it was still there, still solid, still real. She clutched it, trying to remind herself that there was order in the chaos.

But the knock came again, this time from behind her.

She spun around, heart pounding wildly. Nothing. Just the walls. The silence that followed was more terrifying than the sound itself. It meant whatever this was... was no longer outside. Perhaps, it never had been.

Panic gripped her, but not in the way it had the nights she sat with friends, listening to tales in the safety of her village. This was different. Deeper. More insidious. It wasn't just fear of something out there. It was the creeping, paralysing realisation that the true threat might be within …the cabin.

Her mind turned against her, conjuring shapes from shadows, sounds from silence. The cabin became a house of mirrors, every corner distorted by her own imagination. Was this what the old stories meant when they spoke of enchantments in the woods? Not creatures, but confusion. Not monsters, but madness.

She stumbled back onto the cot and closed her eyes, trying to block it all out.

Her thoughts raced wildly between half-formed images of werewolves, shifting shadows, and faceless spirits. She tried to recall the words her grandmother once told her in the middle of a nightmare: "Fear takes root where clarity withers. Tend to your thoughts like you would a garden."

But tonight, her garden had grown wild.

The air grew colder. She wrapped herself tightly in the blanket, still gripping the carved map like a lifeline.

Somewhere beyond the cabin walls, the forest whispered, not in words but in impressions; echoes of thoughts she could not control.

She didn't know how long she lay like that, her eyes half open, heart thudding, breath shallow. It could have been minutes or hours. Eventually, the whispers faded, the shadows receded, and the dread began to loosen its grip.

chapter seven
VII

light in the clearing

A faint light crept through the cracks in the shutters of the cabin, the first signs of dawn. Nia had endured a night of torment, but was unharmed: the fear had not come from the forest. It had come from her.

And now she knew that before she could properly explore the world around her, she would have to confront the one within.

Morning unfurled slowly, as though the forest itself were reluctant to release its hold on the night. Slivers of pale gold filtered through the wooden slats of the cabin, casting a soft glow of light around the furniture in the cabin. Nia stirred at last, her muscles stiff, her mind fogged by the weight of restless dreams and imagined footsteps.

She blinked up at the wooden ceiling, now bathed in the gentle hues of dawn. The oppressive shadows from the night before had melted away, revealing once again the humble warmth of the cabin.

Yet she didn't rise immediately. She lay still for a while, listening to the silence not thick with threat, but alive with the morning's quiet hum. A soft birdsong called from somewhere just beyond the window, and the low rustling of leaves gave rhythm to the new day.

Eventually, she pulled herself upright, glancing cautiously around the room. Everything looked exactly as it had when she arrived, but everything felt different. The lingering dread had softened into something more bearable like the echo of a storm that had passed, leaving a clear sky in its wake.

She approached the window and peered out. The clearing was quiet, bathed in golden light.

The trees no longer loomed; instead, they seemed to stretch gently toward the rising sun, their branches swaying in soft greeting.

And then she noticed something, just beyond the clearing, near the edge of the trees.

Movement.

But this time, it wasn't shadowy or sinister. It was unmistakably human. Two young men, laughing as they unpacked satchels near a feeding horse.

Just outside of the cabin was a large water pot balanced precariously on a flat stone, what must have been the source of last night's eerie creaking and knockings.

Nia watched the strangers for a moment,

Night In A Wood Cabin

both amused and embarrassed. So this was what had stirred her panic? Two travellers and a loose pot? She let out a quiet breath, a soft chuckle slipping from her lips.

She stepped outside into the cool morning air. The earth felt solid beneath her bare feet, grounding her. The forest, in the daylight, had shed its haunting veil and returned to being what it had always been. An ancient, indifferent presence, neither hostile nor hospitable. It simply existed, as it always had.

Tiny creatures scurried between roots, birds darted from branch to branch, and a small squirrel perched on a low branch, nibbling confidently on a fruit. The same creatures that had once loomed like threats in her imagination now seemed small, delicate and charming. The real world had shrunk the monsters that her mind had magnified.

The relief she felt was not just from knowing she was safe, it was the relief of understanding that her fear had been a construct, a narrative woven from myth and memory.

She turned toward the cabin and took one final look at the place that had both sheltered her and tested her spirit. What had once felt like a trap now looked like a teacher. She had wrestled with the darkest corners of her thoughts and emerged not only fearless but wiser.

As she wandered across the clearing, her eyes fell on something carved lightly into the side of the cabin's doorframe—faint, weather-worn, almost imperceptible in the daylight. A small symbol—a spiral, encircled by a sunburst. She hadn't noticed it before. Perhaps it had always been there, or perhaps it had only revealed itself now that she was ready to see it.

chapter eight
VIII

the merchant's lesson

The path back into the woods felt different. Still largely unknown, but it no longer held the weight of menace. It felt expansive. It felt promising.

With her satchel slung over her shoulder and the map still tucked safely inside, Nia walked once more into the forest—this time not as someone seeking escape, but as someone seeking understanding.

The trail welcomed her this time with ease. The same branches that once seemed like grasping fingers now arched above like guardians, letting in shafts of light that danced across the forest floor.

Nia walked calmly now, no longer

flinching at every sound or shadow. Something within her had shifted, not completely transformed, but realigned. Her senses remained alert, but not burdened by fear. The rhythm of her footsteps echoed a new sense of clarity.

As she emerged from the path into a wider clearing, the soft scent of cocoa pods and drying kola nuts drifted toward her. The aroma was earthy and sweet, carrying with it a sense of familiarity. And there he was, the merchant from the day before, crouched beside his woven baskets, sorting fruits with a careful hand.

He looked up and smiled warmly. "Ah,

Night In A Wood Cabin

young adventurer," he greeted. "The forest has not swallowed you whole, I see." Nia returned his smile with a slight laugh. "No," she replied. "Though it tried its best."

He gestured for her to join him. "Sit with me a while. The morning sun makes good company."

She lowered herself onto the woven mat beside him and watched as he expertly sorted the rich, red pods and bitter kola nuts. His hands moved with practised ease, but his presence remained thoughtful and still, as though his movements were secondary to the moment he was sharing with her.

"They are beautiful," Nia said, touching one of the cocoa pods gently.

"They are, aren't they? Here, have one!" the merchant offered, adding: "It took years for me to notice their beauty. I only saw them for the profit they would be traded for at the market."

Both sat in companionable silence for a moment, listening to the breeze rustling through the leaves. Nia breathed deeply, letting the air fill her lungs as she ate.

"I stayed in your cabin," she said softly, almost as if confessing something fragile. "I hoped you would," he replied without looking up.

Nia paused, unsure how to explain the storm of emotions that had consumed her during the night. "It was… peaceful," she began. "But also strange. I was afraid at first. I thought I was being followed. I imagined… creatures in the dark."

The merchant chuckled gently, not with mockery, but with understanding. "Ah, yes. The forest has that effect on many."

"I even thought you might have been a shape-shifting werewolf," she admitted sheepishly. His laughter came freely, deep, warm, and sincere. "Well, I suppose

I've been called worse," he replied.

They both laugh, and in that moment, the tension that had clung to Nia like a shadow seemed to lift completely.

"But truly," she said, "it made me realise how easily fear can twist what we see."

He nodded slowly in agreement. "Fear narrows the mind's vision. It blinds us to the beauty just beyond our focus."

He reached into his basket and pulled out a crimson cocoa pod, studied it for a moment and said. "Let me show you something."

Nia glanced curiously. He motioned towards the forest behind them.

"I want you to look around you now," he said, "but focus only on green. Find every shade of it in the leaves, the moss, the vines. Let your eyes search for nothing else."

Nia did as instructed. She let her gaze travel through the forest, catching every glimmer of green she could find. Light emeralds, deep olives, pale limes and hues of colours she had never truly noticed before now stood out with striking vividness. After a moment, the merchant spoke again. "Now," he said gently, "close your eyes."

Night In A Wood Cabin

She did.

"Tell me," he continued, "what red things did you see?"

Nia paused. "Red?" She questioned, trying to remember. Just… the pod," she said slowly. "Maybe some berries? I don't know."

The merchant smiled knowingly. "Exactly. Now open your eyes and look around."

When she opened her eyes again, to her surprise, red hues were everywhere. She saw berries clinging to vines, flowers peeking from bark, insects with scarlet wings, the glow of the cocoa pods in his baskets.

"I didn't see them," she whispered. "They were there all along, but I didn't see them."

The merchant nodded. "That is how our mind works. What you choose to focus on becomes your reality. You were not blind, you were just looking in a different direction."

Nia let his words settle, reflecting on her adventure so far in the forest.

"Last night in the cabin," she said quietly,

"I only focused on what frightened me. Every sound, every shadow became something monstrous. But it wasn't the forest, it was me."

The merchant smiled again. "You've learned a lesson that many who are older than you never grasp"

She turned to him thoughtfully. "And what about you? Who taught you all this?"

He gazed into the canopy for a moment before answering. "Curiosity. Experience. And a few mistakes too, of course." He stood and offered her a hand. "Come. I must leave for the next village soon."

She took his hand and rose to her feet, still holding the cocoa pod he had given her. "How can I repay you?" she asked. He paused and looked at her with warmth. "Share what you've learned. That's all I ask. The next person who needs a lesson, give it freely to them."

Nia smiled, nodding. "I will."

The merchant gathered his goods, strapped his baskets to his horse's back and rode off to the next village, while Nia continued to explore the woods.

Nia saw herself now under a new

Night In A Wood Cabin

light, no longer as a lost girl, nor as a frightened wanderer, but as a seeker, equipped now with a new lens through which to view the world.

chapter nine
IX

return to the village

Night In A Wood Cabin

The journey home felt different.

The forest had not changed, the trees still whispered in the breeze, the undergrowth still shivered with unseen creatures, but Nia had. The path, which had once seemed so unknowable and vast, now felt familiar. She had walked it before, but this time, she understood it better.

She moved through the winding trails with confidence, not because she knew every turn, but because she no longer feared the unknown. The merchant's lesson lingered in her mind, reshaping the way she looked at the world around her.

What you choose to focus on becomes your reality.

She took in the greens of the leaves, the deep browns of the earth, the speckled golds where sunlight broke through the canopy. She noticed the red now, too, in the berries, the fallen petals, the faint glow of the cocoa pod still tucked in her satchel. Colours that had always been there, waiting for her to see them.

As the hours passed, the landscape slowly shifted. The dense embrace of the woods loosened, the trees thinning into scattered groves, the undergrowth giving way to familiar dirt paths. She was close now.

The sounds of the forest were no longer just nature's hum but interwoven with the distant echoes of village life: laughter, the rhythmic pounding of yams, the occasional bark of a dog.

She felt the weight of her journey settle upon her. She was returning not just with a story, but with something intangible, an understanding of herself that she had not possessed before.

She stepped onto the well-trodden path leading to Ilé-Ifè's market square just as the sun began its descent. The air was thick with the scent of roasted groundnuts, fried plantains, and fresh earth. Traders called out their wares, children darted between stalls, and women balanced baskets of goods atop their heads with effortless grace.

And yet, though the village bustled with the same rhythm she had always known, something felt… different. She had lived in this place her entire life, and yet she now saw it through new eyes.

She passed a group of children gathered around an elder, their wide eyes reflecting the firelight as they listened intently to a story. She caught fragments of something about a tale of a warrior, of a great battle, of a beast vanquished.

She smiled to herself.

She had once listened just as eagerly, absorbing every word, every lesson. But now she understood something deeper, that stories shaped not just the world around her, but the way she experienced it. And perhaps, it was time for a new story to be told.

As she made her way through the village, she spotted familiar faces of friends, neighbours and traders she had seen a thousand times before. Some called out greetings, others gave her curious glances, as if sensing something had changed in her.

Whispers of her return from those who knew her grandmother had been

looking for her reached her home before she did.

When she arrived at her family's compound, the courtyard was quiet, save for the distant sounds of the village. She took a deep breath before stepping inside, the warmth of home wrapping around her like a familiar embrace.

Her grandmother sat by the fire, grinding herbs with slow, steady hands. The old woman looked up as Nia approached, her wise eyes scanning her granddaughter's face.

"You have been away," she said simply, her voice carrying both knowledge and expectation.

Nia nodded. "Yes, Grandmother."

The elder woman studied her for a moment before nodding to herself, as if confirming something she had already known. "And what have you found?"

Nia hesitated. How could she possibly put it into words? The fear, the doubt, the understanding, the shift within her. She thought of the cabin, the merchant, and the forest that had both challenged and guided her.

She reached into her satchel and pulled out the cocoa pod. "Something valuable,"

she said at last.

Her grandmother smiled. "Then sit, child. Tell me everything."

And so, as the stars began to scatter across the night sky, Nia spoke. She told of the forest's eerie whispers, the unsettling presence in the night, the way her own fear had turned shadows into creatures. She spoke of the cabin, of the merchant's lesson, of how she had come to understand the power of perception.

Her grandmother listened, nodding slowly, her fingers still working over the herbs. When Nia finished, the old woman placed a gentle hand on hers. "Fear is like fire," she said. "It can warm you, or it can consume you. The only difference is how you tend to it. You must tend to it…"

"…like you would a garden", Nia concluded softly, letting the word settle deep within her anew.

"You have changed," her grandmother continued. "That is good. But tell me, child… what will you do with this change?"

Nia didn't answer immediately. She looked up at the night sky, remembering how the stars had once seemed distant, unreachable. But now, she saw them for what they were—constant, ever-present, waiting to be noticed. She turned back to her grandmother, a small smile forming.

"I think," she said, "it's time for me to tell a story of my own."

Word spread about how Nia had gone into the woods and came back without being harmed, and a few curious children gathered around her.

One of them asked, "Tell us a story, Nia… tell us about the woods."

She looked at their wide, curious eyes

and smiled. "I'll tell you," she said. "But this is not just a story about dragons or monsters. It's a story about finding courage… when you're alone, in the dark, with only your thoughts for company."

The children leaned in closer as she began, her voice weaving gently through the air like a thread of silk.

And when she finished, the children were filled with wonder. One boy raised his hand. "Is the forest still scary?" he asked.

Nia thought for a moment. "It depends on how you choose to see it," she said.

return to the village 121

"The forest is the same. But we are the ones who experience it differently."

As the fire crackled and dusk settled over the village, the last of the children had gone home, and Nia sat quietly beside her grandmother, watching the flames flicker.

"You've begun telling your stories now," said her grandmother.

Nia nodded. "I think I've always had stories in me… I just needed to walk far enough to hear them clearly."

The older lady chuckled softly, adding, "And what's next for you, my child?"

Nia smiled, her heart alight with a quiet certainty. "Another journey, ma", she said. "Another story."

And somewhere deep in the forest, unseen beneath the moonlit canopy, the cabin stood silently among the trees, waiting for the next traveller who would stumble upon it. Waiting for another tale to unfold.

Because adventure never truly ends — it simply begins again.

The end.

Closing Thoughts

Sometimes, what we imagine in our minds can feel scarier than what's really out there. The unknown can seem big and frightening — but most of the time, it's not as bad as we think. Being brave doesn't mean you never feel scared. It means you choose to face your fear anyway.

A wise thinker once said that fear can stop us from doing the things that make life exciting and meaningful. It can feel like a shadow that follows us, telling us not to try, not to explore, not to dream.

But heroes — like you — don't run away from fear. They take a deep breath, stand tall, and keep going.

When we're bold and take small steps forward, we discover amazing things about the world and about ourselves. We find colour where we thought there was only darkness. We find hope, adventure, and purpose.

So next time you feel scared, remember this: fear is just a part of the journey — not the end of the story.

Scan the QR code to listen to the music soundtrack inspired by this story. Let it guide you, just like the forest did for Nia.

OTHER BOOKS IN THE SERIES

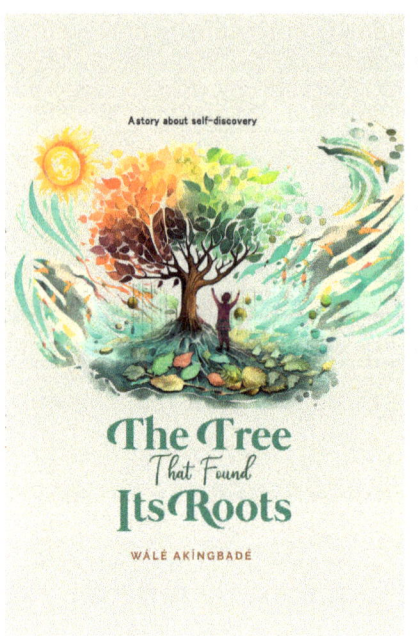

The first book in the Golden Threads of Inspiration series, The Tree That Found Its Roots is an allegorical tale of self-discovery told through the perspective of a tree. It symbolises growth and maturity shaped by relationships and life's experiences. This book introduced the series' beloved characters, whose individual stories inspired the subsequent tales.

"Guided by the wisdom of their father, a hardworking farmer, two brothers embark on a journey that weaves through tradition, culture, and unexpected challenges. Tasked with an errand to the vibrant market of Oja, they face trials that test their integrity, challenge age-old customs, and reveal the true strength of their bond. Journey to Oja is a timeless tale of virtue, growth, and the enduring spirit of a traveller's heart."

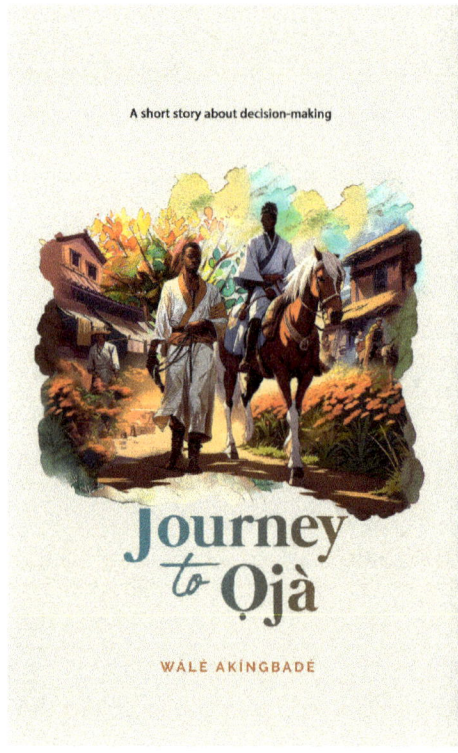

www.ingramcontent.com/pod-product-compliance
Lightning Source LLC
Chambersburg PA
CBHW051601010526
44118CB00023B/2775